Galaxy's Greatest Giggles

by **Matt Rissinger**
and **Philip Yates**

illustrated by **Ethan Long**

STERLING CA

New York / London
www.sterlingpublishing.com

D0188430

To all the students and staff at
the Crossroads School — M.R.

To my brother Eddie — P.Y.

STERLING and the distinctive Sterling logo are registered trademarks of
Sterling Publishing Co., Inc.

Library of Congress Cataloging-in-Publication Data
Rissinger, Matt.
  Galaxy's greatest giggles / Matt Rissinger and Philip Yates.
      p. cm.
  Includes index.
  ISBN 978-1-4027-4255-2
  1. Outer space—Juvenile humor. 2. Wit and humor, Juvenile. I. Yates, Philip, 1956-
II. Title.
  PN6231.S645R57 2008
  818'.5402—dc22
                                    2008003310

10 9 8 7 6 5 4 3 2 1

Published by Sterling Publishing Co., Inc.
387 Park Avenue South, New York, NY 10016
© 2008 by Matt Rissinger and Philip Yates
Illustrations © 2008 by Ethan Long
Distributed in Canada by Sterling Publishing
c/o Canadian Manda Group, 165 Dufferin Street
Toronto, Ontario, Canada M6K 3H6
Distributed in the United Kingdom by GMC Distribution Services
Castle Place, 166 High Street, Lewes, East Sussex, England BN7 1XU
Distributed in Australia by Capricorn Link (Australia) Pty. Ltd.
P.O. Box 704, Windsor, NSW 2756, Australia

Sterling ISBN 978-1-4027-4255-2

For information about custom editions, special sales, premium and
corporate purchases, please contact Sterling Special Sales
Department at 800-805-5489 or specialsales@sterlingpublishing.com.

CONTENTS

3 . . .
2 . . .
1 . . .
LAUGH OFF!

How do you put a baby
astronaut to sleep?
You rocket gently.

How do astronauts
relax in space?
They sit on launch chairs.

What kind of showers do
astronauts usually avoid?
Meteor showers.

Where's an astronaut's favorite
place on the computer?
The spacebar!

Why are astronauts so
impatient on Earth?
Because in space they're wait-less.

Alien space creature #1:
I was born on Jupiter.
Alien space creature #2:
What part?
Alien space creature #1:
All of me, of course!

What do NASA scientists toast around the campfire?
Mars-mellows.

What galaxy is very lowfat?
The Skim Milky Way.

Why did the pig fly into space?
He wanted to be the first ham on the moon.

Dana: My wristwatch is so special,
        it can tell time in the 25th century.
Lana: Now, that's what I call future-wrist-tick.

How did the baby lamb fly to Mars?

By rocket-sheep.

Ben: I'm afraid we'll never see a
full moon again.
Jen: Why is that?
Ben: Because the astronauts brought
part of it back with them.

Brad: The craters on the moon are extremely sad.

Chad: How did you know that?

Brad: Because the teacher says they're depressed.

Mo: Did you hear about the mad scientist who tried to grow a Martian in shaving cream?

Jo: Yeah, talk about alien life foams.

What do you get when you cross a rocket and a sandwich?

Really fast food.

What do you get when you cross a chef and a UFO?

Something that quickly travels through spice.

What did the fault line say to the Earth's crust?

Let's shake on it.

2
Doctor Dillies

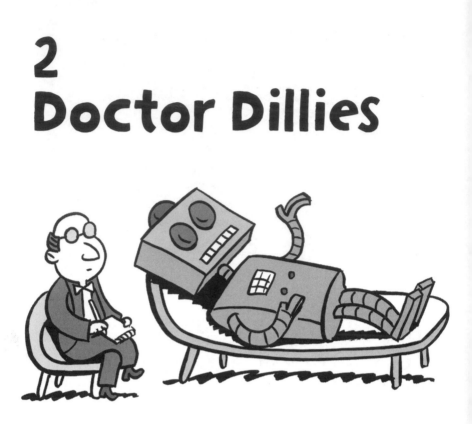

Why did the robot go to a psychiatrist?
He was having a metal breakdown.

Doctor: I wouldn't worry too much
           about talking to yourself.
Patient: But everything I say is boring.

Psychiatrist: Do you have trouble making decisions?
Patient: Well, yes and no.

Doctor: Is that ringing in your ears gone now, thanks to that new medication?
Fuzzy: Yes, but all I get now is a busy signal.

Tex: Doctor, doctor, I think I have walking pneumonia.
Doc: Here, take one tablet every four miles.

Benny: Doctor, what do I do about those aches in my leg?
Doctor: Don't worry; it's just old age.
Benny: But the other leg's the same age, and it feels fine.

Receptionist: Your doctor is out on vacation. Would you like to see Doctor Fudgemabucket?

Patient: Which doctor?

Receptionist: No, he's a real doctor.

Doctor #1 (to Doctor #2):
How is our patient?

Doctor #2:
Not good. Today he thinks he is a fat caterpillar. Yesterday he thought he was a beautiful butterfly.

Doctor #1:
Yes, I see what you mean. He's regressing.

"Doctor, Doctor, I feel like a bungee jumper."
"Well, isn't that stretching it a bit?"

"Doctor, I think I'm a big pecan."
"Well, well. Another nutcase."

Why did King Arthur go to the eye doctor?

He was having trouble with his knight vision.

Phil: I got sick just from reading a
medical textbook.
Jill: Well, I guess that makes you
ill-literate.

Mom: My son thinks he's a smoke detector.
Doc: That's nothing to be alarmed about.

Dad: My daughter thinks she's a refrigerator.
Doc: Don't worry, in time she'll chill out.

How Am I Feeling?

"I need to have my head examined,"
said the cabbage.

"I feel run down," said the car.

"I feel ghastly," said the monster.

"I feel like I have hay fever," said Mrs. Bale.

"No one pays attention to me,"
said the Invisible Man.

"I'm so tired I feel like crashing,"
said the computer geek.

How does a witch-doctor ask someone to dance?
"Voodoo like to dance with me?"

What dentist-turned-rotten-pirate
was very hard to get rid of?
Plaque-Beard.

Lyle went to see his doctor about his compulsive lying. "I can treat you," said the doctor. "But it's very expensive."
"That's okay," replied Lyle. "After all, I just won the $50 million lottery yesterday."

Why did the mosquito go to the dentist?
To improve her bite.

Flo: I crossed an emergency room and a skunk, and guess what I got?
Jo: A medical scenter.

Sunday, Monday, Tuesday, Wednesday, Thursday, Friday, and Saturday went to see their doctor.
"What can I do for you?" said the doctor.
"Well," replied the seven days all at once, "to be honest, we're feeling kind of week."

Patient: Doctor, Doctor, I think I'm a duck. I think I'm a duck.
Doctor: Your problem is that you have a one-quack mind.

What do you get when you cross an acupuncturist and a pine tree?
Someone who's always on pins and needles.

Patient: Doctor, Doctor, I think I'm a banjo.
Doctor: What's wrong with that?
Patient: Everyone keeps picking on me.

Patient: Doctor, I think I'm a bat.
Doctor: I was wondering why you keep hanging around here.

Patient: Do I really need to have a brain transplant?

Doctor: Well, it's time somebody changed your mind.

What did the psychiatrist say when he saw Humpty-Dumpty?

"It looks like he's finally coming out of his shell."

Doctor: Nurse, did you put the patient to sleep?

Nurse: Yes, I told him several of your jokes.

3
Smart Alecks

Dilly: How do you keep your home from freezing in the winter?

Dally: You paint it in the fall and give it an extra coat.

Franny: We bought a house, but it has no water.
Danny: I'll be sure to send you a get well card.

Vinny: Gee, when we moved into our new
house, we found deep holes
in our backyard.
Winny: All I can say is "Well, well, well."

"Help! Help!" the woman screamed into the
telephone. "My house is on fire!"
"How do we get to you?" said the firefighter.
"Probably in those big red trucks you have with
the flashing lights," said the woman.

**Today, everybody watches TV and gets less
exercise. How do you solve the problem?**
Hide the remote control.

Dana: I flipped a coin to find out whether I
should come to your birthday party.
Lana: That was nice of you.
Dana: It wasn't easy, either. I had to keep
flipping the coin until I got it the right way.

Julie: What's the difference between a lemon,
a dinosaur, and a tube of glue?

Louie: I give up.

Julie: You can squeeze a lemon, but you can't
squeeze a dinosaur.

Louie: What about the glue?

Julie: That's where you get stuck on this joke.

What did the jar of paste do on January 1st?

It made a Glue Year's resolution.

Knock-knock!
Who's there?
Satin.
Satin who?
I must have satin some bubble gum.

Lenny: Do you like my new jogging outfit?

Benny: I don't know. Run it by me
once more.

What Do They Do
When They're Angry?

Kettles let off a little steam.
Computers byte back.
Scissors get snippy.
Cars drive you crazy.
Baseball players pitch a fit.

Jason: I split my pants again today.
Mason: Every day it's the seam old story.

Dilly went to summer camp, and on the first day the
camp instructor said, "Every day, I want you to put on
a fresh pair of socks."
Two weeks later, Dilly was a no-show at the flag raising.
Storming into Dilly's cabin, the camp instructor found
Dilly still lying on his cot. "Dilly, why aren't you lined up
with the rest of the campers?"
"How could I?" replied Dilly. "You try putting your
shoes on over fourteen pairs of socks!"

How can you tell if a mime has been talking too much?
He has holes in his gloves.

Dad: How do you like your new horse?
Deirdre: She's terrific. She's very polite.
Dad: What do you mean, "polite"?
Deirdre: Whenever we come to a jump,
she lets me go first.

Clem: I had a growth removed from my head.
Lem: Were you in the hospital?
Clem: No, the barbershop.

**What did one fraction
say to the other?**
"Half a nice day."

Dreams

Why did the fortune teller put a
Ouija board under her mattress?
So she could really dream about the future.

Why did the octogenarian put a
history book under his pillow?
So he could dream about the past.

Why did the little boy put a toy
catalog under his bed?
So he could dream about the presents.

What's worse than a bicycle with no brakes?
Standing in front of a bicycle with
no brakes.

A policeman stopped Henry for driving down
a one-way street. "Where do you think you're going?"
he asked.
"I don't know," replied Henry. "But I think I'm late,
because everybody else is coming back."

Sue: What do you get when you cross
a cowboy with a chauffeur?

Sandy: I don't know, but I bet he's helpful
on cattle drives.

Why did the dweeb driver keep going around and around the block?

Because his turn signal was stuck.

Why didn't the 16 dweebs get into the movies?

Because the sign said "Under 17 not admitted."

Sue: Why did the square girl break
up with the square boy?

Sandy: Because he was
never around.

Did you hear about the two acrobats who got married? They flipped over each other.

Looney Letters to the Rich and Famous

Dear Houdini,
Is it true that the reason you learned to hold your breath under water for so long was because you couldn't swim?

Dear Ben Franklin,
A two-part question: Did your mother really tell you "Go fly a kite"? And were you shocked?

Jill: Do you want to go see the film about two kayakers who fall in love?
John: No, I hate row-mantic films.

Two ladybugs are sitting on a leaf. One turns to the other and confesses: "I'm in love with a firefly."
The other ladybug asks, "But does he feel the same for you?"
"Oh, yes," says the first; "he lights up every time he sees me."

Moe and Joe went camping one summer and discovered there were so many mosquitoes, they had to hide inside their sleeping bags. "Uh, oh," said Joe as he sneaked a peek and saw a swarm of fireflies. "Now we're really doomed."
"What makes you say that?" asked Moe.
"Because now they're after us with flashlights."

Moe: Did you hear about the robot who married a satellite dish?

Jo: No.

Moe: The reception was great!

Patty: I'm sending a get-well letter to my mother.

Maddy: But the envelope is empty.

Patty: As mom always says, "No news is good news."

What do farmers use to guard their prize pumpkins?

Body-gourds.

Answering Machine Madness

Hi, you've reached a classical composer's home. Leave your name and number, and I'll get Bach to you.

This is the psychic hotline. I know it's you, and I'll talk to you later.

This is the time machine inventor. Please leave your name and number, and I'll get back to you yesterday.

You've reached King Arthur's Palace. Leave your name and number, and someone will get back to you to knight.

Hey, you've reached the wolfman. Leave your name and number, and I'll get back to you at a quarter till moon.

Joe: Why did Santa Claus send for his barber?
Moe: To trim the Christmas tree, of course.

What do fish send each other at Christmas?
Christmas cods.

Lana: My wristwatch only
runs every other day.
Dana: I guess it was made
by a part-time employee.

Dora: Even if my watch runs,
I can never tell time.
Nora: Why not?
Dora: Did you ever try to catch up
with a running watch?

4
Tasty Tickles

For a whole month, Tommy walked into a restaurant with a carrot stuck behind his ear. Then, on the 31st day, he came in with a cucumber. The maitre d', who had never questioned why Tommy kept a carrot behind his ear, finally asked, "You've been coming into this restaurant for 30 days with a carrot in your ear, and I never said anything. But now you have a cucumber. What's the big idea?" "It's very simple," replied Tommy. "I couldn't find a carrot today."

Gert: Why are you rubbing mashed potatoes in your hair?

Bert: Mashed potatoes? Darn, I thought it was cauliflower.

Why is a sofa like a roast chicken?

Because they're both full of stuffing.

What do you get when a chicken lays an egg on top of a barn?

An egg roll.

Customer: Does the fried chicken
come by itself?
Waiter: No, I bring it to you.

What do you get when you cross
a fried chicken stand with a
Chinese restaurant?
A place that provides chopsticks to eat drumsticks.

What do you get when you
cross an actor and a baker?
Someone who's always auditioning
for a roll.

Josh: Did you pass pastry cooking class?
Tosh: Yes, with flying crullers.

What do you get when you
cross a baker and a can of pop?
Baking soda.

Molly: You've been counting calories for a month, and you still haven't lost any weight.

Dolly: I know, but at least my arithmetic's getting better.

Worm #1: Do you know a good restaurant?

Worm #2: I know one where we can eat dirt cheap.

The Kookiest Egg Riddle

How do you drop an egg three feet without breaking it?

Drop it from four feet. For the first three feet, it won't break.

What's the difference between a baseball player and food to go?

One takes home plate; the other takes a plate home.

Tiffany: I survived a week in the ocean on just a can of tuna fish.

Melanie: Wow! How did you ever keep from falling off?

Customer: Let me have what that man over there is having.

Waitress: I'll try, but I don't think he's going to be too happy about giving it up.

Customer: Waiter, there's a bug
in my spaghetti!
Waiter: Hold on, and I'll spray it
with pasta-cide.

Floyd: I have a secret tip to eating
the best meal in town.
Lloyd: But you just burned everything
to a crisp.
Floyd: Exactly. Now when Mom comes
home, she'll take me out to dinner.

Customer: Waiter, there's a bee
in my soup!
Waiter: It must be alphabet
soup, because U-C-A-B!

What do you call a dish of ice
cream with a tiny football on top?
A Super Bowl Sundae.

Science teacher: I can take this
ice cream and make an
exact duplicate of it.
Science clown: Hooray, ice cream
clones for everybody!

Knock-Knock!
    Who's there?
Bayou.
    Bayou who?
Bayou an ice cream if
you open the door.

Trey: Waiter, this salad tastes horrible. Are you sure you washed the lettuce?
Waiter: Yes, of course. And if you look hard enough, you can still see the soap on it.

Customer: Waiter, I can't find a single clam in this chowder.
Waiter: Oh, yeah? Well, did you expect to see devils in the devil's food cake?

What manmade object in Asia stretches 4,000 miles, and is made of fruit?

The Grape Wall of China.

Juan: How was that new family-style restaurant you went to last week?
Don: It was kind of fun. My little sister threw a tantrum, and the waitress sent her to bed without any supper.

Mother termite: What would you like for breakfast, Junior?

Son termite: How about a bowl of instant oak-meal?

What's the favorite dessert served at King Arthur's castle?

Pie a la moat.

What would you find in a computer cookie jar?

A chocolate chip.

What would you get if you crossed a camel with a spud?

Lumpy mashed potatoes.

What do you get when you cross donuts and wheat?

Hole-grain goodness.

"Waiter, bring me something to eat, and make it snappy."
"How about a crocodile sandwich?"

5 Animal Crackups

How do you start a teddy bear race?

Ready, teddy, go!

Why is a polar bear so cheap to have as a pet?

It lives on ice.

Tex: What kind of bears like to go out in the rain?

Rex: Drizzly bears.

What is the fiercest flower in the garden?

The tiger lily.

How are tigers like army sergeants?

They both wear stripes.

What do you call a show full of lions?

The mane event.

What happened to the leopard who took a bath three times a day?

After a week, he was spotless.

Which big cat should you never play cards with?

A cheetah.

Why did the fisherman go to the gym?

He wanted to build up his mussels.

What fish discovered America?

Christopher Colum-bass.

How do you download a whale?

First you need a Moby Disk. . . .

How did the skunk call home?

He used his smell phone.

What has antlers and scares people half to death?

Cari-boo.

What do you call a very rude bird?

A mockingbird.

Who was the world's smartest pigeon?

Leonardo Dove-inci.

Why did the chicken cross the net?
It wanted to get to the other site.

What do you give a little chicken on its birthday?
A coop-cake.

What do you call a rooster who wakes you up at the same time every morning?
An alarm cluck!

Why did the turkey cross the road?
To prove he wasn't chicken.

What do you get when you cross an owl and a turkey?
An animal too smart to show up for Thanksgiving.

How long do chickens work?
Around the cluck.

What do you get when you cross
a monkey with a lot of water?
Monkey sea.

What do you get when you
cross a monkey with a little
water?
Monkey dew.

What's the hardest part about taking
baby elephants out for a drive?
Lifting them in and out of their car seats.

Why did the cow cross the road?
To go to the moooooo-vies.

How do cows keep the grass cut?
They use lawn moo-ers.

Why did the beaver go to the hospital?

He was feeling gnaw-seous.

What do you call a cheerful rabbit?

A hop-timist!

Zip: I'm going to buy a ton of goose feathers.

Zap: Are you sure you can afford the down payment?

Valentine's Day Card for Prairie Dogs

I really gopher you.

From a Firefly to His Bride

You light up my life.

What was the snail doing on the highway?

About one mile a day.

What is a snail's idea of an extreme sport?

Trying to outrun a glacier.

How do snails get their shells so shiny?

They use snail polish.

What happened when the dog went to the flea circus?

He stole the show.

What do you get if you cross a dog and a 747?
A jet-setter.

Why did the dog wear white sneakers?
Because his boots were at the shoe repair shop.

What do you get if you cross a dog and a cheetah?
A dog that chases cars—and catches them!

What did the hungry Dalmatian say after he had a meal?
"That sure hit the spots."

What is a dog's favorite food?
Anything that's on your plate.

What do you get when
you cross an elephant
with a sled dog?
A tusky husky.

Why do grocery clerks love dogs?
Because they come complete with
their own bark-code.

What works in a circus, walks a
tightrope, and has claws?
An acro-cat.

What paper is a cat's favorite?
The Daily Mews.

What do you get when you cross a duck with the Abominable Snowman?
Quacked ice.

What's a rabbit's favorite song?
"Don't Worry, Be Hoppy."

What kind of zoo makes the most annoying noises?
A ka-zoo.

6
Jest for Laughs

How did one computer greet the other?

"Hi, Tech."

Where do computer programmers keep their money?

In data banks.

Lloyd: I crossed a car and a leapfrog, and guess what I got?

Floyd: An automobile that jump-starts itself.

Lance: I crossed law enforcement and a pirate, and guess what I got?

Vance: The F. B. Aye! Aye!

Ben: Here's a stumper: What is made of wood but can't be chopped?

Len: Sawdust.

What is the best lawn mower you can buy?

One with good grass mileage.

What did the gardener say
to the compost?

"Thank you very mulch."

Moe: What do you call a tree
with no limbs or trunk?
Joe: I'm stumped.
Moe: That's right.

Career Craziness

Joey: How's your job at the
history book company?

Cloe: It's all right for now, but I
don't see any future in it.

Willy: How's your new job as
a night watchman?

Billy: It's great, but the slightest
noise seems to wake me up.

Steve: I hear you lost your job at
the rubber ball company.

Reeve: Yes. Don't worry,
I'll bounce back.

Jackie: Why is my mail
so soggy?

Postal
carrier: Read the stamp
cancellation. It
says "Postage Dew."

If a red house is made of red bricks, and a blue house is made of blue bricks, what is a green house made of?

Glass.

Willie: Why is the ocean so quiet today?
Tillie: I guess it doesn't have much to spray.

Mia: Did you hear that scientists have discovered a way to duplicate cold cuts?
Tia: No, but it sounds like a lot of cloney-baloney to me.

What did the karate instructor say on December 23?

"Only two more chopping days left until Christmas!"

What time of the year is it when chimneys start sneezing?

Flue season.

Say These Three Times Quickly

The corn on the cob made
Rob's sobbing stop.

Kent sent Trent the rent
to rent Trent's tent.

The ocean sure soaked Sean's
swimming trunks.

How did you get that great job
as a parachute instructor?
Someone pulled a few strings for me.

What game do little
mountains enjoy?
Peak-a-boo.

What is a plumber's favorite movie?
20,000 *Leaks Under the Sea.*

Mo: Did you hear about the new blue jeans that have a calculator sewn into the pocket?

Jo: Yeah, I hear they call them Smarty Pants.

Breaking News

A truck hauling hundreds of chickens just overturned on Highway 5. A lot of chickens crossed the road, but no one has been able to figure out why.

Two bank robbers crashed their getaway car into a cement truck. Police are scouring the downtown area for hardened criminals.

The local lighthouse keeper walked off his job. Everyone's in the dark as to why he quit.

Mo: How did you decide to become
a sewer worker?

Jo: I just sort of fell into it.

What did medieval knights watch on television?

The Knightly News.

What do geologists do for entertainment?

They go to rock concerts.

Why did Frosty have such good self-esteem?

Because everyone told him what an ice job he was doing.

7
Family Funnies

Mark: My dad is taking fish oil
        supplements for his health.
Manny: Does he look healthier?
Mark: I can't tell. He never gets
        out of the swimming pool.

Rudy: My dad was run over by a steamroller.
Judy: Is he in the hospital?
Rudy: Yes, he's in rooms 16, 17, and 18.

Fuzzy: My brother joined the army,
        but he dropped out.
Wuzzy: You mean he left the army?
Fuzzy: No, he's a paratrooper.

Chuckie: I'm homesick.

Buckie: But isn't that your house right over there?

Chuckie: Yes, but I'm sick of it.

What did the grandfather clock say to the baby clock?

"Don't tock back to me!"

What did the daddy snail say to his daughter when he found out she was dating the guy down the block?
"Honey, these long-distance relationships never work out."

"I'll never forget," said Old Man McFurley to his grandson. "We were right in the path of that tornado."
"Was your house damaged?"
Replied Old Man McFurley, "I'm afraid we won't know until we find it."

Mom: Why aren't you going to Juanita's birthday party?
Rhonda: Because the invitation says three to five, and I'm seven.

Wayne: Dad, do you want to buy a fund-raising candy bar for three dollars?
Dad: I thought you said they were just a dollar.
Wayne: They are, but I have to pay for the two I already ate.

A Letter from Camp Couch Potato

"Hey, Ma and Pa . . . wanted to tell you, sofa, so good."

Jake: Hey, Mom, I have absolutely no hang-ups about life.
Mom: Maybe that explains why your clothes are always on the floor.

Willie: For my birthday, my mom's taking me to the West Indies.
Tillie: Jamaica?
Willie: No, we both wanted to go.

Joshua was five and had never spoken a word in his life. None of the doctors his parents took him to had an explanation for this problem.

One day Joshua's mother served him some milk, but Joshua flinched when he tasted it and said, "This milk is sour!"

"It's a miracle," said his parents. "Why have you waited this long to speak?"

Joshua replied, "Well, up until now, everything's been all right."

Chuckie: Dad, you are going to need five dollars in postage stamps to mail this package.

Dad: Do I have to stick the postage on myself?

Chuckie: No, just stick it on the package.

Mom #1: My daughter's grades are making me sick.

Mom #2: It sounds to me like you have bad case of C-sickness.

Mrs. Magilicuddy watched her two sons sledding in the back yard on a snowy wintry day. Concerned at their playing habits, she called the older son in to find out what the problem was. "Jason, I thought I told you to share the sled." "We are sharing," replied Jason. "He plays with the sled going uphill, and I play with it going down."

Mom: How was your history test, Mary?
Mary: Well, I don't really know . . . the questions were easy.
Mom: Well, what was the problem, then?
Mary: The answers were hard.

Mom: Why did you drop out of computer class?
Tom: I just couldn't hack the program.

Dilly: How old is our car, Mom?
Mom: About six years old. Why do you ask?
Dilly: Our teacher wants us to write an autobiography.

Lyle: Our math homework is the first thirty problems in Chapter Six, the next twenty problems in Chapter Seven—

Kyle: All I can say is, "Poor Dad."

Stacy: Mom, which would you prefer, to be run over by a car, or have a bottle of glue spilled all over your best shoes?

Mom: Why, the glue, of course.

Stacy: Thank goodness. Your prayers have been answered.

Husband: My wife talks to the plants.

Counselor: What's wrong with that?

Husband: She's using up all her cell phone minutes.

Where do dads sleep when they camp out?

In pop tents.

Tiffany: Did you know I have three sisters and two brothers?

Melanie: Are you the oldest?

Tiffany: No way. My mom and dad are way older than I am.

Slim: I wish I had listened to my mother.

Jim: What did she tell you?

Slim: That's the problem. I didn't listen.

8
School Daze

Dan: I got an "A" for cutting class.
Stan: What school is that?
Dan: The barbershop school.

Phil: My dog chewed up my homework.
Teacher: What did you do?
Phil: What could I do? I took the words
          right out of his mouth.

Mason: We made bread in home
          economics class, and I
          got a good grade.
Jason: Did they put your name
          on the honor roll?

Toni: Why didn't the clown do well in any of his subjects in school?

Joni: Because he had a fun-track mind.

Teacher: What can you tell me about the Iron Age?

Class clown: Sorry, I'm a little rusty on that.

What do they take at school that only matters if you're missing?

Attendance.

What do you get when you cross an absent-minded professor and a truck driver?

Someone with bad short-turn memory.

How did the baseball player who never opened a book get through school?

The teachers just let him slide.

What kind of tests do bungee cord jumpers enjoy?
True or falls.

Teacher: Bobby, use the word "insulate"
in a sentence.
Bobby: Every morning you ask me,
"Why did you come insulate?"

Teacher: What one word do you always
pronounce wrong?
Student: I don't know, what?
Teacher: "Wrong."

School nurse: How bad are your
sleeping problems?
Student: So bad that I haven't been
able to sleep in class for
three weeks.

Science teacher: Johnny, what is
a satellite?
Johnny: It's what a cowboy turns
on when it gets dark.

In school, who is doubly funny?
The class clone.

Why did the gardener take a
class on how to talk to plants?
Because he always wanted to learn
a fern language.

Why did it take the parrot
so long to graduate?
He kept repeating each year.

While attending astronaut school, Benny was asked by his teacher: "If you were on a deserted planet and you were facing the North Star, what would be on your right?"

"East, ma'am."

"Correct," replied the teacher. "Now what would be on your left?"

"West," said Benny.

"Correct, again. Now, finally what would be at your back?"

Benny thought carefully for a moment and replied: "Well, ma'am, that would be my oxygen tank."

Teacher: The space shuttle can do every thing a bird does, correct?

Class clown: I dunno. Can a space shuttle lay eggs?

Teacher: Why does it take 75 hours to get to the moon?

Class clown: Because it's uphill all the way.

English teacher: This essay you wrote about your dog is the same as your sister's.

Student: Well, of course—we have the same dog.

Judy: My history teacher talks to himself.
Rudy: Does he realize it?
Judy: No, he thinks we're listening.

Teacher: The noise is so loud in here,
            I can't hear myself speak.
Clown: Don't worry. You're not
            missing anything.

"Baxter," said the teacher, "you've been sent to detention every day of this week. What do you have to say for yourself?"
"There's only thing to say," said Baxter. "I'm glad it's Friday."

Mom to principal: This school is terrible.
                     I'm going to get my
                     son transferred.
Principal: But your son is getting
                     straight A's.
Mom: That's how I know this
                     school is terrible.

Our school is so serious about grades, even in the cafeteria the eggs and the butter have to be Grade A+.

If football teams have cheerleaders,
do ice hockey teams have chill-leaders?

| Teacher to student: | Are you sleepwalking in class? |
| Student (yawning): | Well, didn't you say to follow your dreams? |

| Teacher: | For bonus points . . . what happens in leap year? |
| Class clown: | I don't know, but I'm happy I have an extra day to figure it out. |

Why were Santa's helpers sent to the school guidance counselor?

Low elf-esteem.

Sign on the School Nurse's Office

Ouch to lunch.

Bill: Did you pass your mile-run test in gym?

Phil: I passed, all right. Passed out after twenty feet.

Teacher: Spell "sleep."
Class clown: S-L-E-. . . .
Teacher: What comes next?
Class clown: Dreaming about summer vacation.

How do you become a zookeeper without going to school?

Take a course on-lion.

Teacher: Please spell "ginger ale,"
"root beer," and "sarsaparilla."

Student: Oh, no, not another pop quiz!

Bob: I got in trouble, and my parents sent me to a child guidance center.

Barb: How did it go?

Bob: Not so good. Those kids were really no help at all.

Nerd #1: Why are you wearing a hat with a compass on it?

Nerd #2: I was told my life needed direction.

Teacher: What state manufactures the most trousers?

Class clown: Pants-ylvania.

You know your summer vacation is off to a bad start when . . .

They close the pool because of icebergs.

On TV you see an ad that says, "It's never too early to shop for back-to-school clothes."

Your talking alarm clock says, "Get up; it's only April."

Your best friend has the mumps and isn't allowed out of the house until September.

9
Wiggly Giggles

How do you start an insect race?

One, two, flea–go!

What did the clean dog
say to the insect?
Long time, no flea.

Rudy: I collect fleas as a hobby.
Judy: And how do you spend your time?
Rudy: Scratching.

How do you find where a flea
has bitten you?
Start from scratch.

What insect runs away from
everything?
A flea.

What is the difference between
a flea and a wolf?
One prowls on the hairy, and the other
howls on the prairie.

If there are five flies in the kitchen, how do you know which one is the American football player?
He's the one in the Sugar Bowl.

What did one firefly say to the other?
"Got to glow now!"

Jon: How do we know that insects are clever?
Don: Because they always know when you're eating outside.

What is an insect's favorite game?
Cricket.

What has antlers and sucks blood?
A moose-quito.

What is a mosquito's favorite sport?
Skin-diving.

What has six legs, bites, and talks in code?
A Morse-quito.

What does a caterpillar do on New Year's Day?
Turns over a new leaf.

Teacher: What is the definition of a caterpillar?
Class clown: A worm in a fur coat!

How can you tell which end of a worm is which?
Tickle it in the middle and see which end laughs.

Why did the sparrow go to the library?
It was looking for bookworms.

What did the woodworm say to the chair?
"It's been nice gnawing you."

What is the best advice to give a worm?

Sleep late.

What is life like for a termite?
Boring.

Which bug gobbles up trash?
The litterbug.

What do you call an insect with frog legs?

An ant-phibian.

Who is the most famous French ant?

Napole-ant.

What kind of ant is good at arithmetic?

An account-ant.

What medicine would you give a sick ant?
Anti-biotics.

What do you call a 100-year-old ant?
An ant-ique.

What did the spider say when he broke his new web?
"Darn it!"

What's the biggest moth in the world?
A mam-moth!

What do you get if you cross a firefly and a moth?
An insect who can find its way around a dark wardrobe.

What did the spider say to the fly?
"Let's get married and have a big webbing."

Spider 1: You seem anxious
and upset.

Spider 2: Well, I've been climbing
the wall all morning.

Why are spiders such good swimmers?

They have webbed feet.

Why are spiders like tops?

They are always spinning.

Rich: What do you call a bee
that can't make up his mind?

Mitch: A may-bee.

What is a baby bee?

A little humbug.

What did the bee say to the naughty bee?

"Bee-hive yourself."

What did the bee say to the other bee in summer?

"Swarm here, isn't it?"

What goes hum-choo, hum-choo?

A bee with a cold.

Why did the queen bee kick out all of the other bees?

Because they kept droning on and on.

What do bees do if they want to use public transport?

Wait at a buzz stop.

Who is a bee's favorite classical music composer?

Bee-thoven.

Why was the centipede dropped from the insect football team?

He took too long to put his cleats on.

What is worse than an alligator with a toothache?

A centipede with athlete's foot.

What do you call a guard with 100 legs?

A sentry-pede.

Why was the centipede late?

Because he was playing "This Little Piggy" with his baby brother.

What do you get if you cross a centipede and a chicken?

Enough drumsticks to feed an army.

10 Calling All Monsters

Why do dinosaurs wear glasses?
To make sure they don't step on other dinosaurs.

What's red on the outside and green on the inside?
A dinosaur wearing red pajamas.

Lenny: What did the man say when he saw the dinosaurs coming down the path wearing sunglasses?
Benny: Nothing! He didn't recognize them!

What dinosaur loved to pile up pancakes?

Stack-a-saurus.

Stan: Did you hear about the ten tons of woolly mammoth hair that was stolen from the wig-maker today?
Dan: No, I didn't.
Stan: The police are now combing the area.

What should ghosts always wear on the beach?
Sun scream.

What's a ghost's favorite story?
"Boo-ty and the Beast."

Why aren't ghosts good liars?
Because you can usually see right through them.

What do you get when you cross Robin Hood and a ghost?
Someone who is good with a boo and arrow.

How did the yeti feel when he had the flu?
Abominable.

What kind of TV would you find in a haunted palace?
Wide-scream TV.

What was the Abominable Snowman's favorite childhood game?

Freeze tag.

After having his creature jolted by lightning, around the lab Dr. Frankenstein often referred to his monster as old Watt's-His-Name.

What did Dr. Frankenstein say when he got hit by lightning?

"That's what I get for brainstorming!"

Jill: When I snap my fingers, it keeps space monsters from coming to Earth.
Phil: That's funny; I haven't seen any space monsters.
Jill: See? It works!

How do monsters keep their breath clean?

They gargoyle twice a day.

Dilly:　What do you do with a green monster?
Dally:　You wait until it ripens.

Godzilla discovered her son eating an entire football team. "What's the big idea?" said Godzilla to her boy. "I thought I told you to share everything."
"Oh, all right," said Baby Godzilla. "How about I give you a halfback?"

Kyle:　Just imagine you were on Jupiter and some space monsters were trying to kill you. What would you do?
Lyle:　I would stop imagining right away.

Knock-knock!
    Who's there?
Athena.
    Athena who?
Athena alien spacecraft fly by.

Flip: How does a space creature count to 20?
Flop: On one of its hands.

What happens when a ghost haunts a theater?
The actors get stage fright.

What dinosaur loved collecting old bottles and cans?

Recyclo-saurus.

About the Authors

Matt Rissinger and Philip Yates are the founders of National Knock-Knock Day, celebrated each year on October 31. Their other books include *Cleverest Comebacks Ever, Totally Terrific Jokes, Greatest Jokes Ever, It's Not My Fault Because..., Best School Jokes Ever, World's Silliest Jokes,* and several more. Philip is the author of a picture book, *A Pirate's Night Before Christmas,* also published by Sterling.

Matt lives near Valley Forge, Pennsylvania, with his wife, Maggie, daughters Rebecca, Emily, and Abigail, their dog, Breaker, and cat, Cleo. Philip lives in Austin, Texas, with his wife, Maria, and their two cats, Sam and Johnnie.

Visit www.laugh-a-roni.com for more jokes and to learn even more about Matt and Philip and their work.